# Cultivating Resilience

## *Overcoming Adversity through Effective Communication*

# Table of Contents

# Chapter 1. Introduction

In a world where turbulence and unpredictability seem to be the order of the day, we're delighted to present to you our special report, "Cultivating Resilience: Overcoming Adversity through Effective Communication." This illuminating exploration is not merely a guide but an optimistic journey, crafted with the intent to inspire readers to cultivate resilience within themselves and their communities. Dwell into revealing insights that transform adversity into a forge for character, harnessing the power of effective communication. Expect to be motivated and empowered as you discover tactful, precise, and compassionate communication strategies that have helped individuals and teams alike to bounce back from life's unexpected setbacks. Seize this opportunity to learn, adapt and thrive, no matter what life throws at you. This report is your roadmap to resilience, illuminating the path that leads to a happier, more robust, and resilient you. Engage with us on this enlightening journey and welcome an era of personal growth and effective communication.

# Chapter 2. Understanding the Power of Resilience

Resilience is more than just a buzzword; it is a critical quality that proves essential in various aspects of life. In the face of life's constant trials, one constant remains: resilience, the ability to recover from setbacks, adapt well to change, and keep going in the face of adversity. The importance of resilience cannot be overstated. Having the strength to stand firm in the face of adversity is an attribute we all can cultivate. Let's begin our exploration of resilience by understanding its power.

## 2.1. The Essence of Resilience

Resilience is the mental, emotional, and physical ability of individuals to effectively deal with adversity, change, stress, and challenges. It is about bouncing back, but it's also about growth. It means cultivating the ability to keep moving forward, even when the going gets tough, by harnessing strength, optimism, and adaptability.

It's crucial to remember that resilience is not about suppressing pain or pretending that everything is fine when it isn't. It's about being fluid, adjusting to new situations, and learning from the process of overcoming adversity.

## 2.2. Identifying Resilient Traits

Everyone possesses resilience to varying degrees. However, recognizing and honing the traits that contribute to it can significantly enhance this quality within us. Some common qualities of resilient individuals, which could be present inherently or learned through experiences, include:

- Emotional Awareness: Understanding one's emotions and the emotions of others.

- Optimism: Believing in positive outcomes despite the challenges.

- Self-Efficacy: Trusting one's own abilities to get things done.

- Flexibility: Successfully adapting to change and new circumstances.

- Solid Problem Solving Skills: Being able to think of effective solutions to difficult situations.

Moving forward, it's essential to understand that these traits are not static. They can be nurtured and developed, offering opportunities for personal growth and greater resilience.

## 2.3. The Impact of Adversity on Personal Growth

Adversity and hardship are often seen negatively, but when viewed differently, they can be transformative, leading to profound personal growth. Every challenge comes with valuable lessons that encourage growth and resilience, both professionally and personally.

Adversity throws the rule book out the window, forcing individuals to adapt and improvise. It presses us beyond our comfort zones, allowing us to experience new perspectives and ideas. This expansion can be a valuable catalyst for personal growth, ultimately expanding our locus of resilience.

## 2.4. Harnessing Resilience for Overcoming Challenges

No one is immune to life's downsides and challenges. Individuals and communities worldwide face trials and misfortunes every day, and resilience plays an integral role in overcoming these.

Resilience helps individuals confront their fears, reduce anxiety, move past roadblocks, and heal from trauma. By building resilience, people can take life's harshest experiences and turn them into opportunities for improvement and change.

It's essential to remember that building resilience doesn't mean making the problem disappear; it means strengthening yourself to handle and move beyond the problem. Resilience enables individuals to navigate through various life challenges, gaining strength and wisdom in the process.

# 2.5. Building Resilience: A Step-by-Step Guide

Understanding the power of resilience sets the foundation for the next step: building resilience. While the process of cultivating resilience may vary from person to person, some general guidelines apply:

1. Get Connected: Building strong, positive relationships with loved ones is fundamental to building resilience. Emotional support can be a powerful tool in maintaining resilience in the face of adversity.

2. Embrace Change: Seeing change as an opportunity, rather than a threat, is a vital part of resilience.

3. Practice Self-Care: Physical health plays a significant role in resilience; you cannot maintain mental stamina without caring for your physical wellbeing.

4. Cultivate a Positive Mindset: Deliberately focusing on the positive aspects can boost emotional resilience.

5. Foster Purpose and Determination: Having a clear sense of

purpose can steer you in the right direction and help you stay on track when adversity strikes.

# 2.6. Enhancing Resilience through Effective Communication

Effective communication is a powerful tool in the resilience-building toolbox. It nurtures relationships, helps share perspectives and clears misunderstandings - all of which are necessary for building resilience.

Moreover, empathetic communication can foster deeper connections, allowing for greater emotional support during tough times. It can also pave the way for conflict resolution, leading to less stress and greater resilience in the face of adversities.

Communication can be a powerful tool to convey our experiences and emotions, which aids in the process of healing and resilience-building. By being vocal about our struggles and fears, we open the door for support, understanding, and empathy, making it easier to bounce back from setbacks.

By understanding the power of resilience, we are taking the first step towards cultivating it within ourselves and our communities. Resilience is more than just an innate trait; it is a skill that can be nurtured and honed to effectively overcome life's obstacles, growing stronger with each challenge we overcome. It is indeed the key to transform adversity into a forge for character.

# Chapter 3. Decoding Adversity: A Deep Dive

Adversity is often pictured as a dark cloud, uninvited and unwelcomed, obscuring the sunlight of happiness and prosperity. However, adversity, more often than not, is simply a test of mettle, a crucible meant to refine and not break, a stepping stone rather than an immovable rock. As we initiate this immersive deep dive into decoding adversity, the key is to shift our perception, acknowledging adversity's inherent potential for growth and transformation.

Adversity isn't necessarily an endpoint; it's a waypoint, a place of embarkation from where we must set sail, propelled forth by the winds of resilience.

## 3.1. Unwrapping the Enigma of Adversity

Adversity isn't unilateral but a multidimensional concept with various facets. It often comes in gusts of financial difficulties, health crises, loss of loved ones, professional hurdles, or catastrophic events. Each form of adversity brings along unique challenges that require distinct coping strategies. To effectively deal with adversity, it's crucial first to understand outright what you're dealing with. Acknowledge the situation, label the emotions accompanying it and then gear up for the journey ahead. Remember, preparing is not losing, but gaining a foresight that can turn the tide in your favor.

## 3.2. The Impact of Adversity on Mind and Body

Adversity takes a toll on both our mind and body, inducing outwardly signs of stress like a fast beating heart, excessive sweating, and insomnia, while internally, it can lead to anxiety, depression, and heightened emotional sensitivity. Chronic exposure to adversities can also trigger negative health outcomes such as cardiovascular disease and weakened immunity. Thus, the battle isn't just about bouncing back from adversity but also ensuring we safeguard our physical health amid the chaos.

## 3.3. The Psychology of Coping

Our psychological response to adversity is crucial in carving our path towards resilience. Persons posing a 'challenge' mindset eying adversity as an opportunity for personal growth and learning withstand blows better than those with a 'threat' mindset, who view adversity as a danger. Leveraging techniques from cognitive-behavioral therapy could help us foster a 'challenge' mindset, thus altering our perception of adversity.

## 3.4. Strategies for Fostering Resilience

Resilience is not an inborn trait but a skill to be mastered. The key to becoming resilient lies in developing a supportive social network, maintaining a positive view of oneself, accepting that change is a part of life and fostering traits like optimism and tenacity. It's like building muscles - continuity, even with small steps, wins the race.

## 3.5. Harnessing the Power of Effective Communication

Communication emerges as a pivotal tool in overcoming adversity. Within oneself, it takes the form of self-talk, shaping perceptions and guiding actions. In a group, it serves as the glue, strengthening bonds, fostering teamwork, and instilling confidence. Effective communication paves the way for empathy, understanding, and shared problem-solving, going a long way in mitigating the impacts of adversity.

## 3.6. Embracing the 'New Normal'

Adversity often thrusts us into a 'new normal,' forcing us to adapt to the altered circumstances. Whether it's navigating a physical disability post-accident or establishing a life after financial bankruptcy, the 'new normal' requires acceptance, modification, and adaptation. Acknowledging and accepting this new normal is the first and most critical step towards effectively dealing with adversity.

## 3.7. The Role of Tech and Digital Tools

In today's world, digital tools and platforms can play a critical supportive role in overcoming adversities. Applications and virtual platforms offer resources for stress management, cognitive behavioral therapy, and foster a sense of community among individuals experiencing similar adversities. Distance is not an issue in the digital world; support is always a click away.

## 3.8. Future Forward: From Surviving to Thriving

Conquering adversity is not about merely surviving or getting past the setback; it's about thriving and arriving at a point of growth that was unimaginable before. This transition requires courage, endurance, and patience, with the promise of a more robust, self-aware 'you' at the horizon. The idea is to metamorphose the raw experience of adversity into a gem of wisdom and strength.

As we conclude this deep dive into adversity, let us then not shy away from this unwelcome guest. Instead, let's acknowledge and engage with it. Let's understand it for what it truly is - an opportunity for metamorphosis and growth, and a stepping stone to a bolder, brighter future.

# Chapter 4. The Mechanics of Effective Communication

Communication is the lifeblood of our society, its importance transcending the constructs of time, place and culture. Effective communication penetrates even the hardened walls of adversity, imparting resilience and facilitating a common understanding. Let us begin by delving into its fundamental mechanics before taking a more profound exploration of its lesser-known aspects.

\n === Understanding the Basics

\n Effective communication is not merely about conveying a message. It's about ensuring the desired understanding is achieved. This process involves two crucial components: the sender and the receiver. The sender initiates the conversation by creating and sending a message, laden with their thoughts, emotions, and intentions. The receiver, on the other hand, intercepts and decodes this message, integrating it with their existing knowledge and perceptions.

\n For the communication process to be effective, clarity and accuracy are paramount. A clearly articulated and well-conveyed message helps prevent misunderstandings and misconceptions. This doesn't mean one needs the eloquence of a seasoned orator, but a clear understanding of their thoughts and emotions and the ability to express them genuinely and coherently.

\n === The Role of Active Listening

\n Contrary to popular belief, communication isn't a one-way street. Active listening is a vital and often overlooked part of the process. It involves not just receiving the words spoken, but interpreting and understanding the entire context of the communication. Paying attention to non-verbal cues, maintaining eye contact, nodding to encourage the speaker, refraining from interruption, and offering applicable responses are all proponents of active listening. This not only fosters better understanding but also validates and acknowledges the sender's perspective, making them feel heard and valued.

\n === Non-Verbal Communication: Reading Between the Lines

\n Non-verbal cues arguably convey more than the words uttered. Tone, inflection, facial expressions, body gestures, eye contact, and even the pace of speech - all paint a picture more comprehensive than words ever could. Being aware of one's non-verbal cues and learning to interpret those of others significantly enhances the effectiveness of communication.

\n A gentle nod might reinforce agreement, while a furrowed brow could indicate confusion. Attention to these silent aspects can potentially rectify misunderstandings before they arise, making for smoother, more effective interactions.

\n === The Power of Empathy

\n While understanding is essential, empathy brings forth the human aspect of communication. It entails viewing the situation from the other person's perspective, respecting their feelings, and validating their experiences. Empathetic communication fosters trust, understanding, and connectivity, making it an invaluable tool in fostering resilience amidst adversity.

\n === Overcoming Communication Barriers

\n Barriers are inevitable in communication. These can come in many forms - physical, linguistic, cultural, even emotional. The key to effective communication lies in not just recognising these barriers but also in adopting strategies to overcome them.

\n Empathy again plays a significant role in helping recognize and transcend interpersonal barriers by creating a safe space for open dialogue. On occasions when the communication gap is due linguistic or cultural differences, taking the time to learn and understand the other party's language or culture can be immensely beneficial.

\n === The Art of Feedback

\n Feedback is a critical closing loop of communication, offering a space for the sender to know how their message was received, and for the receiver to clarify, ask questions, or contribute their ideas. Constructive feedback can be a powerful tool for personal and professional growth, while also serving to enhance the effectiveness of future communications.

\n Whether it's a simple confirmation of understanding, a suggestion for improvement, or even a word of appreciation, feedback should be clear, concise, and open, thus making it a critical player in effective communication.

\n Each of these elements pieced together creates a holistic picture of effective communication. Like a well-oiled machine, each cog needs to be in place, working in perfect synergy for the process to run smoothly. However, mastering these mechanics is not a one-time process. It's a journey of learning and adapting, continually evolving with time and experience.

\n Cultivate these tools of communication, and watch as they unlock doors to resilience and understanding, turning adversity into a stepping stone towards growth and success. Let this not be an end, but the commencement of your journey towards mastering the art of communication for resilience.

# Chapter 5. Hidden Connections: Resilience and Communication

Resilience, often regarded as a personal attribute, has broader ripple effects that impact the community as a whole. It is a dynamic and evolving process necessitating continuous engagement and adaptation – a process deeply rooted in communication. But the importance of communication in cultivating resilience is frequently understated.

## 5.1. The Resilience Communication Interface

Resilience and communication are intricately interwoven phenomena. Regardless of the inherent resilience levels, without effective communication, the potential to navigate adversity significantly reduces.

Think about a tree with a robust root system, symbolizing inherent resilience, while the exchange of nutrients to various parts of the tree portrays the role of communication. As resilient as the root system might be, without the continuous communication (nutrient exchange) between roots and branches, the tree cannot survive a storm's brunt. The journey of resilience is similar, and communication serves as the conduit that strengthens one's ability to withstand, adapt to, and recover from adversities.

Communication acts as a catalyst to resilience in three essential ways:

- **Information Sharing** – Proper communication ensures a steady flow of critical information,a basis for making informed decisions on adapting to situational changes or overcoming adversities.

- **Emotional Support** – Expressing feelings and thoughts during turbulent times provides emotional relief and fosters mental resilience.

- **Social Cohesion** – Regular interaction strengthens societal bonds, making communities more resilient to wider adversities.

# 5.2. Understanding Communication for Resilience

In the resilience journey, the first step is acknowledging that processing adversities is complex and demands a profound understanding of the communicational aspects. The clues to resilience are often buried within these interactions. Several forms of communication help in enhancing resilience.

- **Intrapersonal Communication:** The conversation one has within one's mind significantly influences the resilience levels. The narratives one constructs about oneself, experiences or adversities determine the manner of response to adversities.

- **Interpersonal Communication:** It's a two-way process involving the exchange of messages between individuals. This contact helps in sharing experiences, support, and strategies to adapt, which forms the bedrock of collective resilience.

- **Mass Communication:** Media outlets and technology platforms allow invaluable information flow during adversities, guiding individuals and societies to equip themselves better.

# 5.3. Cultivating Resilience through Effective Communication

Creating a more significant impact requires the ability to communicate effectively, which is a teeming blend of clarity, empathy, and adaptability. As one navigates through life's adversities, the capacity to communicate meaningfully enhances resilience significantly.

1. **Clarity:** Communication is effective when the intended message is clear and well understood. It becomes a powerful resilience tool by equipping individuals with necessary comprehension to handle situations head-on.

2. **Empathy:** Empathetic communication can provide emotional assurance and support, fostering individual and collective resilience.

3. **Adaptability:** Communication styles evolve based on circumstances. Adapting gracefully to these changes increases resilience.

# 5.4. Enhancing Communication: Tools for Building Resilience

Various tools can aid in honing your communication skills, whose practical application can result in marked improvements in your resilience.

- **Active Listening:** Effective communication begins with active listening. It is an art that facilitates a deeper understanding of the other person's perspective, fostering resilience as a result of improved mutual understanding.

- **Expressive Writing:** This form of communication enables individuals to vent suppressed emotions and reflect on their experiences. It not only provides catharsis but builds resilience by helping an individual to process their feelings.

- **Storytelling:** This is a powerful way to share experiences, lessons, and strategies for resilience. Sharing stories of resilience through adversity also inspires and serves as a guide for others on similar journeys.

- **Digital Communication Tools:** The Internet age has resulted in a plethora of digital tools aimed at enhancing communication. Social media platforms, blogging sites, forums, and groups are platforms for informational exchange and support systems, creating more resilient individuals and communities.

The journey towards resilience is not easy. It involves pain, struggle, growth, and, most importantly, learning. It is a dynamic process that relies heavily on effective communication. This association appears invisible but significantly impacts the capacity to withstand and bounce back from life's predicaments. Embrace communication as a resilient tool, creating a more robust and adaptable self, ready to face any adversity that life may present.

# Chapter 6. Case Study Analysis: Resilience through Communication

Adversity: it's an omnipresent facet of life, an inevitable rite of passage that everyone must face. However, unique in their approach and galvanized through effective communication, some individuals and organizations manage to not just endure adversity, but thrive in its wake.

## 6.1. The Power of Communication

Profound and effective communication, both internal and external, can act as a bulwark against adversity, fostering resilience and encouraging growth. When confronted with a crisis, the way an individual or organization communicates can dramatically impact its capacity to navigate through the storm.

Internally, communication shapes the way we perceive the world, our circumstances, and ourselves. Negative internal dialogue can limit our potential, keeping us mired in adversity. Conversely, positive self-communication can inspire hope, foster determination, and energize our pursuits.

Externally, communication plays a critical role in mediating relationships, managing crises, and embracing opportunities. Open, compassionate, and clear communication with others can ease tensions, clarify misunderstandings, and encourage collaborative problem-solving.

# 6.2. Metaphor of River Rafting: A Case in Point

The stream of adversity can be likened to an untamed river for individuals and organizations. Take river rafting as an analogy. In harsh wilderness, with unpredictable currents and sudden obstacles, effective communication becomes the glue holding the team together. Subtle cues and clear instructions shared among team members can spell the difference between trouble and triumphant progression.

Resilience built on effective communication is evident in this context, with trust, balance, and team dynamics hinging on this intricate dance of words and signals. Deciphering rapids, managing movements, and coordinating actions depend on clear, confident communication. Thus, teams conquer adversity, not through avoiding obstacles but engaging with them, communicating with precision and empathy, turning challenges into shared victories.

# 6.3. Individual Case Study: The Story of John

John was a man facing adversity in its rawest form. Having lost his job amid an organizational downsizing, John's world seemed to collapse. He was cloaked in sentiments of failure, uncertainty, and fear. Negative self-talk, a form of internal communication, had cemented his perspective of being a victim to circumstances, thus limiting his outlook.

John decided to flip the script. He started to consciously reshape his internal dialogue, replacing negative narrative with motivating and empowering self-talk. This switch in internal communication, from victimhood to empowerment, rejuvenated his mindset. John harnessed this resilience to venture out, network with peers, and explore job opportunities, a testament to his cultivated resilience.

Interestingly, John's renewed internal dialogue began reflecting in his external communication. His interactions with potential employers became more confident, his articulation of skills and past experiences more eloquent. It wasn't long before John landed a role that afforded him growth and satisfaction, underscoring the hand-in-glove relationship of effective communication and resilience.

# 6.4. Organization Case Study: The Company Y's Transformation

The global financial crisis of 2008 hit Company Y hard, sending shockwaves through its operations. Many predicted Y's demise as their stocks plummeted, and faith in leadership waned. Navigating these treacherous waters required more than just financial acumen; it needed a new communication approach that would rekindle faith, stimulate solidarity, and hence foster resilience.

To weather this storm, the leadership of the Company Y initiated open dialogues with employees, shareholders, and stakeholders. Internally, the management strived for transparency, sharing the reality of the situation along with a strategically crafted recovery plan. This clarity quelled rampant speculation and restored faith among employees, thus fostering internal solidarity.

On the external front, Company Y focused on reassuring stakeholders and sharing their comprehensive plans publicly. The consistent, honest communication, coupled with demonstrated perseverance, won over the wavering trust of investors and stakeholders.

With these revamped communication strategies, Company Y managed to navigate the harsh economic conditions and foster resilience within its ranks. Within the next two years, the company's stocks rose, and operations were back to full efficacy, a testament to the resilience cultivated through effective communication.

# 6.5. Tools and Techniques

The right tools and techniques can significantly enhance communication practices. Techniques such as mindful listening, empathy, assertiveness, and concise messaging are pivotal in establishing effective communication. Digital tools, on the other hand, facilitate organization-wide communication, ensuring everyone is on the same page, fostering collaboration, and assisting in crisis management.

In essence, communication is an irreplaceable tool for resilience during times of adversity. Mastering this skill allows one to transform challenges into opportunities, creating a more constructive narrative about oneself and overcoming adversities. This exploration should inspire you to recalibrate your communication strategies, fostering resilience and effectively navigating through the tribulations of life. Remember, it's not the adversity we face, but how we respond to it that truly defines us. Empower yourself, bridge gaps, and create a more resilient world through the power of effective communication.

# Chapter 7. From Words to Actions: Communication Techniques for Resilience

Developing resilience, particularly in the face of life's more challenging and discouraging moments, requires a proactive approach. This entails not just adapting to adversity but transforming it into a source of personal and collective strength. A critical facet of this process, often overlooked, is communication. Communication underpins all our interactions, whether personal, professional, or communal. Thus, leveraging effective communicative techniques can be profoundly impactful in bolstering resilience.

Understanding, employing, and refining these techniques empowers us to not just articulate and understand our experiences, but also navigate through them with greater ease and efficiency. This chapter, therefore, offers detailed insights into several such techniques, rendered with real-world examples, practical exercises, and research-backed evidence for a holistic comprehension and application.

## 7.1. The Power of Self-Talk

Self-talk, the internal dialogue that continuously murmurs in our minds, significantly influences our perception. From our responses and emotions to our actions and reactions, self-talk sets the tone. Hence, transforming this self-talk to be more affirmative and constructive can profoundly influence our resilience quotient.

One effective approach to this is reframing, a cognitive-behavioral technique that involves reinterpreting negative or adversarial situations in a positive or neutral light. For instance, instead of thinking "I failed," consider shifting it to "I learned something new."

In practice, keep a journal to document your daily thoughts, especially those that recur. Review these entries and identify any negative thoughts or themes that emerge. Then, practice reframing each negative thought into a positive one.

Another important aspect of self-talk is self-compassion. Contrary to being overly critical or harsh on ourselves, it's essential to speak with kindness and understanding. In the face of adversity, remind yourself that difficulties are a part of life, and it's completely okay to fall—we just need to pick ourselves up and move forward.

## 7.2. Non-Verbal Communication: A Silent Dialogue

Non-verbal communication, often overshadowed by its verbal counterpart, is incredibly powerful in conveying emotions and intentions. It entails all non-linguistic elements like body language, facial expressions, posture, and tone of voice.

Recognizing and refining our non-verbal cues helps ensure consistency between our verbal and non-verbal messages, thereby enhancing our authenticity and influence. Practice mindful listening—an attentive and empathetic approach that involves focusing on the speaker and responding to their non-verbal cues. This not only ensures that everyone feels heard but also fosters an atmosphere of mutual respect and understanding.

## 7.3. Appreciative Inquiry: Focusing on the Positive

Appreciative Inquiry, a model developed by Cooperrider and Srivastva, focuses on identifying and amplifying an organization or individual's strengths rather than weaknesses. From a resilience perspective, it fosters a feeling of empowerment and harnesses positivity even in the throes of adversity.

The model works on a 4-D cycle: Discover (identify positive characteristics), Dream (envision a future where these characteristics are magnified), Design (chart a course to achieve this dream), Destiny (implement the course of action). Thus, it ensures a forward-thinking and sustainable approach to resilience.

In practice, conduct a personal or group Appreciative Inquiry session. Facilitate a dialogue on past successes, what enabled them, and how they can be reproduced or enhanced in the future. This method is effective in building resilience in both individuals and communities.

## 7.4. Active Constructive Responding: Cultivating Positive Relationships

A concept developed by psychologist Shelly Gable, Active Constructive Responding (ACR), focuses on how we respond to others' good news. By reacting positively and constructively, ACR enhances relationship satisfaction and fosters a supportive and encouraging atmosphere—important factors in developing resilience.

Practice incorporating ACR into your interactions. When someone shares good news, show genuine interest, ask details, and celebrate with them. Avoid passive or destructive responses, which can dampen enthusiasm and establish a negative communication pattern.

## 7.5. Difficult Conversations: Navigating with Skill and Empathy

Difficult conversations are inevitable. By approaching them with skill and empathy, these can be converted into opportunities for growth and understanding. Aim to approach these conversations with an open mind, focusing on the issue at hand, not the person.

To successfully navigate challenging dialogs, employ the DESC (Describe, Express, Specify, Consequences) model. Start by Describing the situation objectively, express your feelings, specify the changes required, convey the consequences if the change is or is not implemented. Practice using this model in low-stakes scenarios before employing it in more challenging conversations.

In conclusion, effective communication is more than mere information transmission. It's about understanding and being understood; it's about compassion, tolerance, and empathy. Moreover, it's about transforming communication from a mere exchange of words into a potent tool of resilience. Through adoption and practice of these techniques, one can cultivate an environment of positivity, growth, and resilience, gearing up to seize life's challenges as opportunities for growth.

# Chapter 8. Cultivating Personal Resilience: A Pathway to Triumph

The cultivation of personal resilience is a voyage of self-discovery and personal growth. A journey filled with trials, triumphs, heartbreak, and renewal. It necessitates intentional efforts, an unfaltering spirit, and a willingness to embrace adversity. Though resilience is often perceived as difficult to teach, it can be harnessed through dedication and persistent practice. This chapter aims to provide a detailed exploration into strategies for fostering personal resilience and utilising adversity as a pathway towards triumph.

## 8.1. Understanding Resilience

Resilience can be defined as the ability to recover or bounce back from stress, adversity, or hardship. It's the rubber ball effect – to spring back into shape after being stretched, compressed or distorted. It is important to understand the definition and attributes of resilience, as it provides a mental framework to build and implement resilience strategies in our own lives.

A resilient mindset is characterised by optimism, understanding of personal abilities, emotional regulation, problem-solving skills, and the ability to sustain social relationships. Every person has inbuilt resilience, though its intensity may vary. Cultivating resilience involves navigating these attributes effectively and building them into regular habits.

## 8.2. Harnessing Adaptability and Optimism

Resilient individuals exhibit a high degree of adaptability. They are able to reframe challenges, viewing them as opportunities to learn and grow. A proactive approach to dealing with life's uncertainties can help in fostering a resilient mindset.

Optimism is another key trait of resilient individuals. Studies have linked optimistic outlooks with better physical health, lower levels of depression, and longer lifespans. Remember, your perception decides your reality. A glass half full, instead of a glass half empty, is more than a cliché. It guides the manner in which you interpret and respond to life situations. Cultivating optimism can be as straightforward as maintaining gratitude journals, practicing mindfulness, or spending time in positive, supporting environments.

## 8.3. Developing Emotional Intelligence

Emotional intelligence is the ability to understand, use, and manage emotions in positive ways to communicate effectively, empathise with others, overcome challenges, and defuse conflict. Emotional intelligence plays a significant role in resilience, as understanding one's emotional reactions can assist with mitigating stress and promoting positive interactions with others.

Ensure you follow the four key steps to enhance emotional intelligence: identifying emotions, using emotions to facilitate decision-making, understanding emotional meanings, and managing emotions. Tools, such as meditation and journaling, can facilitate this process.

# 8.4. The Power of Positive Relationships

Nurturing positive relationships can greatly support personal resilience. Emotional support from family, friends, mentors, colleagues, and communities helps us maintain a positive outlook and consistently strive towards our goals.

Engage with people who inspire positivity in you. Participate in group activities that promote mutual support, empathy, and understanding. Share your thoughts, stories, and feelings with people you trust. These interactions nourish personal resilience and provide the necessary emotional tenacity to bounce back from adversities

# 8.5. The Art of Self-Care

Self-care shouldn't be overlooked when attempting to cultivate resilience. Personal care and restoration are vital to maintaining a resilient mindset. Exercise, a balanced diet, and ample sleeping hours are fundamental pillars in the cultivation of personal resilience. These elements not only benefit physical health but also enhance emotional wellbeing, foster a positive mindset, and increase resilience towards stress and adversity.

Consider techniques like yoga, meditation, and deep-breathing exercises to manage and mitigate stress. Take proactive breaks when you need to recharge and never underestimate the rejuvenating power of nature.

# 8.6. Building Resilience through Effective Communication

At the heart of building resilience is the ability to communicate effectively. Skilful communication helps one manage and express emotions, establish and nurture relationships, solve problems, and overcome conflicts. It assists in bridging gaps in understanding and enables individuals to seek and offer assistance when needed. Being able to express vulnerability, empathize with others, provide genuine constructive feedback or lessen conflicts are all hallmarks of effective communication that can bolster resilience.

## 8.7. Review and Reflect: The Continuous Learning Journey

Remember, the journey of cultivating resilience is a continuous evolutionary process. Your resilience will be tested; it is through these tests that it will be strengthened. As you utilize these strategies to cultivate your personal resilience, it is vital to regularly review and reflect on your progress. Reflect on the strategies you've implemented and the results they've produced. Lessons can be found in every triumph and setback. Transform these learnings into wisdom by applying them proactively in your daily life thus setting up a cyclic feedback loop that will constantly drive you to improve, adapt and thrive.

Having resilience doesn't mean you won't experience difficulty or distress. It's not about avoiding stress but learning how to thrive within stress. The real power of resilience lies in harnessing stress to bring out your best potential, rather than viewing it as a dreaded nuisance. Move beyond the narrow notion that resilience is merely the capacity to endure. It's the courage to grow from challenges and the wisdom to view adversity as a pathway to triumph.

# Chapter 9. Fostering Resilient Teams: The Role of Communication

Building and maintaining a resilient team is an essential ingredient for success in modern organizational life. It requires continual effort, determination, and most crucially effective communication. Effective communication ensures that everyone on the team is on the same page and understands not just what they are doing but why they are doing it. It also paves the way for an open and supportive environment that breeds resilience and encourages individuals to overcome challenges together.

## 9.1. The Foundation of Resilient Teams

The resilience of a team is seated in its ability to withstand and recover from adversities. Teams face numerous challenges including variations in workload, rapid organizational changes, and unexpected setbacks. A resilient team, however, is not characterized simply by its ability to absorb these blows and still perform its tasks. It is a team that uses adversity as a springboard, learning from these experiences, growing stronger and more cohesive in the process.

The foundation of such a team is cemented with trust, mutual respect, shared responsibility, and most significantly, effective communication.

## 9.2. The Role of Effective Communication

One of the key elements that carves resilience into teams is effective communication. It reduces misunderstandings that can lead to conflict, builds trust and mutual understanding, increases employee engagement, and encourages teamwork and cooperation.

Effective communication binds the team together, allowing them to unite in the face of adversity and come out stronger on the other side. Open and transparent communication channels relay necessary information swiftly and accurately, which in turn helps teams make better decisions even under high-stress situations.

## 9.3. Building Trust Through Communication

Trust is the bedrock of resilient teams. It is generated through open, clear and honest communication. It allows team members to rely on each other even under tough conditions. Trust is not a one-time venture but must be nurtured regularly with sincerity.

Clear and consistent communication by leadership fosters a trusting environment where a team member can comfortably voice their ideas, concerns or questions, without fear of ridicule or sanction. This continuous transparent interaction not only builds trust but also encourages individuals to share knowledge and contribute to the team's resourcefulness.

## 9.4. Ensuring Mutual Understanding

Mutual understanding within a team ensures that all members are equipped with relevant information needed to fulfill their roles effectively. This understanding is accomplished through concise and clear communication. Understanding sometimes means perceiving and relating to another person's emotional state as well.

Effective communication establishes a mutual understanding that helps members interact better, function efficiently, and adapt to ongoing changes. A resilient team is one which communicates adeptly to reach a mutual understanding, thus fostering a sense of belonging and solidarity amidst the team members.

# 9.5. Developing Shared Responsibility

Shared responsibility promotes a sense of ownership and accountability among team members. It encourages members to give their best, knowing that the success of the team hinges on the collective efforts of all its members.

Communication is the cornerstone of cultivating shared responsibility. Regular dialogue about goals, expectations, and individual roles in achieving these targets is vital. In addition, an open communication environment where team members can hold each other accountable in a cordial manner helps foster resilience.

# 9.6. Promoting Psychological Safety

One of the significant traits that resilient teams possess is psychological safety. This refers to an environment where individuals can express their thoughts, ideas, and concerns without fear of punishment or rejection. Communication plays an important part in building this safe space.

Frequent team conversations, dialogues, discussions, and positive feedback can help. A team with a consistent communication structure promotes the practice of "listening to understand," an important factor behind psychological safety.

# 9.7. The Path Forward

Resilient teams are built over time. The journey can be long and winding, with setbacks and obstacles. However, by consistently employing effective communication, organizations can create an environment that nurtures team resilience. This will ensure that teams can face challenges with less fear and more confidence, always ready to bounce back stronger than before.

Clear, transparent, and empathetic communication can turn a team into a tightly bound unit, capable of withstanding adversity and primed for long-term success. This transformative power of communication brings teams together, creating meaningful connections among team members and making them more engaged and invested in their work.

Employing purposeful communication techniques isn't a one-time task but an ongoing process, a long-term investment. It is this investment that carves resilience and adaptability into the heart of teams, turning them into strong pillars that uphold organizational success, even in the face of unprecedented adversity.

The potential to foster team resilience lies in every interaction, every conversation, every communication effort made within an organization; the key is to recognize this potential and utilize it to maximum effect. This report is your supportive companion in that journey towards cultivating resilience through communication. So, do not wait. Start now. Communicate, connect, unite. Foster resilience today.

# Chapter 10. Resilience and Communication in Leadership

Leadership is often synonymous with inherent qualities such as decisiveness, vision, and the ability to motivate a team. However, resilience, and its close cousin, effective communication, are arguably the two most critical attributes for a leader in this ever-evolving world. Let's dissect these qualities and explore how they empower leaders to navigate life's most turbulent waters.

## 10.1. Understanding Resilience in Leadership

Resilience is more than just the capacity to bounce back from adversities; it is about growth and evolution. In the context of leadership, resilience can be described as the leader's ability to sustain their team's morale and productivity amid setbacks and challenges, all the while learning from these experiences and growing stronger.

Chuck Palahniuk, the renowned American novelist, explained resilience aptly, "only after disaster can we be resurrected." Leadership demands that individuals embrace their struggles and transform them into stepping stones for growth. This transformation is not limited to personal development but extends to the team or organization they lead.

For a resilient leader, adversities are not roadblocks but detours on the path to success. These leaders embrace discomfort, look at challenges through the lens of integrative complexity, and embody a growth mindset that helps them to adapt, evolve, and flourish in the face of obstacles. They arm themselves with unwavering optimism, balance their emotional responses, encourage open dialogue, and promote a culture of learning from failure.

## 10.2. The Integral Role of Communication

Effective communication in leadership is integral but often underestimated. A resilient leader is an effective communicator who understands how to relay messages with clarity, empathy, and respect.

Effective communication fosters understanding, trust, and a sense of security among team members. It enables leaders to convey their vision, expectations, and feedback clearly, leaving no room for ambiguity. Good communication helps in conflict resolution and promotes a healthy work culture where all team members feel valued and heard.

When leaders practice effective communication, they encourage openness. Open communication leads to better team collaboration and problem solving. It promotes innovation and creativity, as employees feel comfortable sharing their ideas without fear of retaliation.

When there is turbulence, it's the leader's message that reassures the employees and restores balance. Through honesty and transparency, leaders can maintain team morale even in uncertain times. This includes not only sharing what is happening and why but also actively listening to employees' concerns and suggestions.

# 10.3. Resilience and Communication: The Synergy

Resilience and communication in leadership are mutually reinforcing. Good communicators are often resilient, and resilient leaders often excel in communication.

Resilient leaders effectively communicate a vision of resilience: they persuasively articulate that challenges are integral to growth, implicitly framing adversity as an ally and not an enemy. In doing so, they instill the same resilience in their teams, enabling them to move forward with determination and hope.

When adversity strikes, these leaders use communication to normalize the struggle, share the lessons learnt, and rally their teams towards resilience. They genuinely listen and empathize with their team's struggles, fostering an environment of emotional wellbeing and collective resilience.

In challenging times, clear and honest communication instills trust and alleviates escalating group anxieties. It ensures that the team is unified and that every member is acknowledged. This unity and acknowledgment fuel resilience, collectively and individually.

# 10.4. Practical Strategies for Cultivating Resilience and Communication

1. Foster a Growth Mindset: Promote a culture where mistakes are perceived as opportunities for learning and growth.

2. Practice Emotional Intelligence: Balance your emotional responses and encourage others to do the same. Use empathy in your communication.

3. Prioritize Transparency: Practice open communication, sharing not only triumphs but also failures, and foster an environment of trust.

4. Encourage Active Listening: Show genuine interest in your team's input and be responsive to their feedback.

5. Normalize Adversity: Frame adversity not as a catastrophe but as a part of the growth journey.

By integrating resilience and effective communication in their leadership style, leaders can foster robustness within their teams, thereby transforming their teams and organizations into citadels of resilience. In the new normal that is characterized by ambiguity and unpredictable challenges, resilience and effective communication become vital survival tools for any leader wishing to succeed.

# Chapter 11. Championing Adversity: Your Roadmap to Resilient Communication

In the face of adversity, communication can either serve as a lifesaver or tie us down like an anchor. Recognizing the power that words and interactions wield can transform intimidating obstacles into stepping stones towards resilience and growth.

## 11.1. Your Voice: An Instrument of Resilience

Your voice is more than a mere audible representation of your thoughts; it is an instrument of resilience. It is through your voice that you can share your personal story, convey your emotions, and connect with others. When used wisely, this instrument can become a conduit for resilience, an avenue for psychological growth, a pathway to healing, and a bridge to connectedness. Learning to communicate with authenticity and openness can undoubtedly empower you to better understand, navigate, and ultimately rise above the challenges that come your way.

Consider this scenario: A young woman is faced with an unexpected job loss. How she communicates her story following this setback plays a significant role in her resilience journey. If she frames and shares her narrative from a perspective of victimhood, she may likely convince herself and others that she's incapable of overcoming these circumstances. In contrast, if she tells her story by highlighting her ability to endure and recover from this setback, she can cultivate an atmosphere of resilience – in her own life and those around her.

# 11.2. Dismantling Miscommunication: The Fortress of Clarity

In the realm of adversity, miscommunication becomes an unwelcomed ally that fuels confusion, misunderstandings, and stress. It's important to dissect each part of conversation - the words spoken, the message received, and everything in between. Considering verbal, non-verbal, and para-verbal communication as interconnected can lead us to clearer, more effective communication, in turn constructing a fortress of resilience against adversity.

To dismantle miscommunication effectively, the first step is to ensure that your messages are expressed clearly and explicitly. Ambiguous communication not only fuels misinterpretation, but it also deprives the recipient of the opportunity to provide the necessary support and assistance. Simply put, clearer messages are more likely to be understood, acknowledged, and acted upon.

# 11.3. Listening: The Silent Component of Communication

When we think of resilience-building communication, we often overlook the silent element – listening. However, active listening plays a vital role in effective communication. It involves genuinely focusing on the speaker, understanding their message, showing empathy, and providing thoughtful response.

Active listening invites trust, respect, and mutual understanding – ingredients of resilient relationships, which are foundational for overcoming adversity. It promotes better problem-solving approaches by ensuring a comprehensive understanding of the situation, thereby aiding in fortifying resilience.

# 11.4. Nurturing Empathy: The Emotional Nexus

Empathy is a powerful tool in our communication toolkit. It brings about connections on an emotional level, binds us together through shared experiences, and fosters an environment where individuals feel seen, heard, and understood. By nurturing empathy in our communication, we create an emotional nexus through which we can negotiate adversities effectively.

Communicating with empathy involves shifting from a self-centric perspective to incorporating others' emotions and experiences. This allows you to understand their situations more accurately, relate to their feelings sincerely, and offer more effective and appropriate responses. An empathetic communicator is often regarded as a pillar of strength, which is essential during times of adversity.

# 11.5. Navigating Diverse Communication Styles

Understanding and navigating diverse communication styles can pave a smooth roadmap for increasing resilience. Different people perceive and process information differently and express themselves in numerous ways. Having the ability to understand this diversity will ensure that your message is delivered constructively and received effectively.

Whether these styles are influenced by culture, upbringing, or personal preferences, a resilient communicator views them as an opportunity rather than an obstruction. Adapting your communication can help overcome misunderstandings, improve relationships, and consequently, enhance your resilience towards adversity.

# 11.6. The Growth Mindset: Embracing the Challenge

When it comes to resilience, your mindset plays a vital role in shaping your communication. Embracing a growth mindset, which is characterized by the belief that abilities and talents can be developed through hard work, opens up pathways to resilience.

In the context of communication, a growth mindset can make an enormous difference in how adversities are framed and addressed. Rather than seeing obstacles as insurmountable setbacks, a growth mindset enables you to view them as challenges that can be overcome through persistent effort, learning, and adaptation. Your communication evolves from utterances of defeat to dialogues of learning and progress.

In conclusion, communication is not merely about transmitting information but about fostering resilience. In adversity's face, resilient communication is like a lighthouse, guiding you through the stormy seas towards safer shores. Use your voice wisely, dismantle miscommunication, master the art of listening, nurture empathy, appreciate diverse communication styles, and embrace a growth mindset. These are the signposts on your roadmap to resilient communication. Identify them, understand them, and leverage them to champion adversity, build resilience, and contribute to the growth of yourself and those around you.